Barack OBAMA

Barack OBAMA

WORKING to Make a DIFFERENCE

Marlene Targ Brill

Ⓜ Millbrook Press • Minneapolis

Photographs courtesy of © Timothy A. Clary/AFP/Getty Images, p. 2; © Robyn Beck/
AFP/Getty Images, p. 6; © Tom Bean, p. 9; © Charles E. Rotkin/CORBIS, p. 11; © Yann-
Arthus-Bertrand/CORBIS, p. 13; © G. E. Kidder Smith/CORBIS, p. 14; © Joseph Sohm,
Visions of America/CORBIS, p. 16; AP/Wide World Photos, pp. 18, 37; © Co Rentmeester/
Time Life Pictures/Getty Images, p. 20; Punahou School Archives, pp. 22, 23;
Occidental College Archives, p. 25; © Ralf-Finn Hestoft/CORBIS, p. 28; © Thomas
Mukoya/Reuters/CORBIS, p. 31; © Steve Liss/Time Life Pictures/Getty Images, p. 33;
Special Collections Department, Harvard Law School Library, p. 34; © Nam Y. Huh-
Pool/Getty Images, p. 39; © Kevin Winter/Getty Images, p. 40; © John Gress/Reuters/
CORBIS, p. 42.
Cover photograph: © Nancy Kaszerman/ZUMA Press.

Millbrook Press, Inc.
A division of Lerner Publishing Group
241 First Avenue North
Minneapolis, MN 55401 U.S.A.

Website address: www.lernerbooks.com

Library of Congress Cataloging-in-Publication Data

Brill, Marlene Targ.
    Barack Obama : working to make a difference / by Marlene Targ Brill.
        p.   cm. — (Gateway biographies)
    Includes bibliographical references and index.
    ISBN-13: 978-0-8225-3417-4 (lib. bdg. : alk. paper)
    ISBN-10: 0-8225-3417-7 (lib. bdg. : alk. paper)
    1. Obama, Barack—Juvenile literature. 2. African American legislators—
Biography—Juvenile literature. 3. Legislators—United States—Biography—
Juvenile literature. 4. United States. Congress. Senate—Biography—Juvenile
literature. 5. Racially mixed people—United States—Biography—Juvenile
literature. I. Title. II. Series: Gateway biography.
E901.1.O23B75 2006
328.73'092—dc22   2005016298

Manufactured in the United States of America
2 3 4 5 6 7 – BP – 11 10 09 08 07 06

CONTENTS

Family Tree 8

Different Lands 16

School Years 20

Off to College 26

Pounding the Pavement 27

Family in Kenya 30

New Directions 32

Public Office 35

Going National 38

Important Dates 43

Glossary 45

Further Reading 46

Acknowledgments 46

Index 47

Thousands of supporters held up Barack Obama signs to cheer on the U.S. Senate candidate from Illinois during the keynote address he gave at the Democratic National Convention in July 2004.

A tall, thin man stood before thirty-five thousand cheering fans. He was running for U.S. senator from Illinois. But tonight the Democratic Party asked him to speak at their 2004 national convention. This was a huge honor for a newcomer to politics. Television, newspapers, and radio were broadcasting the event. Soon the entire nation would learn about the talented man with big ears and an unusual name. They would meet Barack Obama.

Obama waited calmly for the crowd to quiet. His eyes twinkled. His usual sparkling smile spread from ear to ear. As he scanned the crowd, he thought about how interesting it was that someone from a divided home was up here making a speech aimed at healing a divided nation.

Finally, the clapping faded. In a strong voice, Obama introduced himself and said how unlikely a keynote speaker he was. He told about his parents and grandparents, half from distant lands. He recounted their different cultures and their hardships. More important, he recalled their common dreams for their children. They held high hopes for a better life in America. They felt pride in what

America could offer its citizens. "I stand here knowing that my story is part of the larger American story," he said.

Obama talked about America's problems too. Some government leaders hoped to split the country by wealth, race, or religion. Divisions only smothered dreams and hurt families, he said. Instead, he called on Americans to join together to make dreams come true for every parent and child.

"I say tonight . . . there's not a black America and white America and Latino America and Asian America. There's the United States of America. In the end, that is . . . (the) greatest gift to us, . . . the bedrock of this nation; the belief in things not seen; the belief that there are better days ahead."

When Obama finished, the flag-waving crowd roared. Cameras flashed. The future senator had moved an entire nation with his message of hope. Where did these words come from? Who was this powerful voice who joked about being a "skinny guy with a funny name"?

Family Tree

The seeds of Obama's beliefs were planted during his multiethnic upbringing. "It was a wonderful childhood in the sense that I saw the world very early," he told a *Chicago Sun-Times* reporter.

Barack was born on August 4, 1961, in Honolulu, Hawaii. His mother, Stanley Ann Dunham, was a white woman from the Midwest. His father, Barack Obama, was a black man from Africa. They named their baby Barack, meaning "blessing from God."

"My name comes from Kenya, and my accent comes from Kansas," the younger Obama liked to explain.

Barack's roots spread far and wide. On his mother's side alone, family history blended antislavery Kansans and Cherokee Indians with Scottish and Irish blood. Stanley Ann's birthplace in Wichita, Kansas, lay in the heart of the United States. People from Kansas in the 1940s were generally plainspoken and hardworking. Many worked for local oil companies or farmed corn.

Grassy plains stretch across most of Kansas. Barack's mother, Stanley Ann, grew up in this heartland state.

When Stanley Ann was born, her father, also Stanley, wanted a son. But the child turned out to be a girl. Always stubborn, Stanley gave the baby his name anyway and added the Ann. Stanley Ann grew up after World War II (1939–1945). The middle 1940s was a time when the country took great pride in its tough soldiers. Strict rules guided most treatment of girls and boys. A manly name for a female triggered terrible teasing. Playmates called the little girl Stanley Steamer and Stan the Man. Stanley Ann soon dropped her first name and kept the Ann.

Cornfields and oil rigs provided Ann's father with his first jobs. But he kept searching for better work. Ann's mother, Madelyn Dunham, supplied the common sense in the family. But she couldn't keep her restless husband in one place for long. The family moved often. They lived in Texas and then Seattle, Washington. Stanley sold furniture or found other odd jobs.

After Ann finished high school in Seattle, the family left for Hawaii. The group of islands were about to become the fiftieth state. Honolulu, the capital, bustled with new hotels and stores. The first jet had taken off from the island, returning with sun-loving tourists. The possibility of unlimited opportunity lured Stanley to the growing city. He took another job selling furniture.

The steady sunshine, spotless beaches, and views of the towering Diamond Head crater suited the Dunhams. They moved to a street with huge Chinese banyan and monkeypod trees. Once settled in their home, Stanley and Madelyn set out to find other freethinkers like themselves.

An aerial photograph of downtown Honolulu taken in the 1960s includes the giant Diamond Head crater rising in the distance while waves crash on the sandy shore.

Honolulu offered a mix of people from nations throughout the Pacific Ocean. The Dunhams met Hawaiians from the islands. They also met neighbors with roots in Japan, the Philippines, and China, and whites like themselves from the U.S. mainland. No one ethnic group claimed a majority of the population. Honolulu encouraged the mix of people. The city name means "a joining together," *hono*, and "shelter from the wind," *lulu*. Government leaders nicknamed their hometown the Gathering Place.

Ann enrolled in the University of Hawaii. During her first year, she took a class in Russian language. Here the shy eighteen-year-old girl met a tall, dark foreign student. She soon fell in love with the stately Barack Obama.

Obama was born into the Luo people of Kenya. The tribe was known for its smart people who often entered politics. His father, Hussein Onyango Obama, was tribal elder and medicine man. But the British ran Kenya as a colony at the time. Hussein worked as a cook for British officers throughout most of his son's childhood.

Obama spent his early life in a poor village along Lake Victoria. He herded his father's goats. Wild antelope, hippos, and lions wandered nearby plains. Once old enough, Obama attended an English-speaking school in a tin-roof shack. The colonial government had set up these schools around the country. From the beginning, his sharp mind stood out in class. With time, he earned a scholarship to a better school in Nairobi.

While Obama studied in Nairobi, Kenya gained independence from Great Britain. Kenyan leaders established a joint education program with America. The Kenyan government sent the nation's most promising students to U.S. universities. The students contracted to return to Africa with the latest information. That way, Kenya could become a modern nation.

Twenty-three-year-old Obama was chosen to attend the University of Hawaii. In 1959 he became the school's

Barack Obama, who was later to give his name to his son, grew up in a Kenyan village similar to this one on the shore of Lake Victoria.

first African student. He studied economics and earned top grades. He became well known for speaking out on behalf of other foreign students. Together they formed the International Students Association with Obama as the first president.

Ann Dunham met Barack Obama of Kenya in class at
the University of Hawaii (above).

While in Russian class, he was drawn to the easy-
going, intelligent Ann. They debated politics and the
economy together. They talked about terrible clashes over
race in the United States. Southern whites expected blacks
to sit in the back of buses and use separate bathrooms.
Many towns stopped blacks from voting and blacks and
whites from dating each other. Protests erupted across the
South. Obama never understood the inequality in such a
great nation. Even Kenyans had earned the right to walk
with whom they wanted and go where they pleased.

As they talked, the two grew closer. Ann invited
Obama home to meet her parents. Madelyn and Stanley
easily took to his charm and quick mind. Ann and

Obama married in 1960, a bold move. Half the states in the country banned mixed marriages. In much of the South, if the couple traveled as husband and wife, Obama could be hung. But Ann and Obama adopted the color-blind model that Hawaii represented.

The newlyweds lived with Stanley and Madelyn while they finished school. Within a year, little Barack, nicknamed Barry, was born. Now that they were grandparents, Madelyn and Stanley preferred the names Gramps and Toot, the Hawaiian word for "grandmother." From the beginning, they doted on their grandson. But a baby strained the family finances. Madelyn found a job as secretary for a bank to help pay the extra bills.

Two years later, Barry's father graduated. He completed a four-year program in three years and came out at the top of his class. Harvard University gave him a scholarship to continue his education. There was one hitch, though. The school offered just enough money to cover one student. Ann and the baby had to stay behind.

After Harvard, Barry's father returned to Kenya. He had a duty to the country that sent him overseas. He also had responsibility for his Kenyan wife and children. As was Luo custom, he could marry more than one woman as long as he cared for them and their children. Barry's parents divorced.

For years, Barry knew his father through old photos and family stories only. His grandparents fed him tales of his father's brilliance and commitment to bettering the world. His mother reassured him that his brains came from his father. Even with these stories, many questions about his father nagged at Barry as he aged. Ann, Gramps, and Toot showered Barry with love. Still, he felt something unexplained was missing in his life.

Different Lands

Barry grew up much as a Hawaiian American boy. He ate sashimi (sliced raw fish), poi (taro root paste), roast pig, and rice candy with wrappers that could be eaten. He learned to swim and body surf in the shimmering blue green and purple waters off Sandy Beach. His grandfather took him to see astronauts land at Hickam

Barry grew up on the Hawaiian Island of Oahu, which is ringed with sandy beaches.

Air Force Base. They went spearfishing at Kailua Bay.

When Barry turned six, his world totally changed. His mother married another foreign student from the university. This time, her new husband was an Indonesian named Lolo. Lolo had been coming to the house for the last two years. He was shorter than Barry's father, and he had thick dark hair and an easy smile. Barry found Lolo to be a calm man who made time to wrestle with him and play chess with Gramps. Barry and his mother were going to Jakarta, the capital of Indonesia, to live with Lolo.

After arriving in Indonesia, Lolo drove them past villages that faded into forest and boys riding water buffalo in a brown river. Tiny stores and one-storied white-washed homes lined the dirt road leading toward Lolo's house. The family's first house was at the edge of town. Barry went from a big-city home in Hawaii to a small, open red stucco-and-tile house that bordered a jungle. The backyard fenced in squawking chickens and ducks, a large beige dog, two birds of paradise, a white cockatoo, two baby crocodiles, and a pet gibbon named Tata.

Moving to Indonesia seemed like a great adventure to Barry. His first night in the new home, Barry watched Lolo's servant lop off the head of a chicken for their welcome dinner. Later, Barry slept under a mosquito net in the open house. He fell asleep to the sound of chirping

OBAMA SAYS HIS FAVORITE BOOK as a child was *Where the Wild Things Are* by Maurice Sendak.

Barry included stories from his childhood in his autobiography, *Dreams from My Father*.

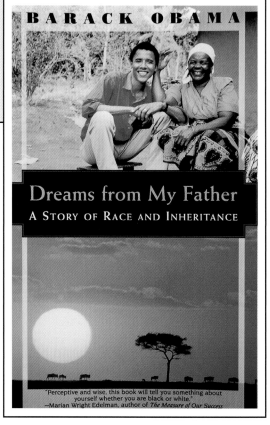

crickets. "I could hardly believe my good fortune," he remembered in his autobiography, *Dreams from My Father*.

Lolo worked as a geologist, and Ann taught English at the U.S. Embassy. When together, Lolo treated Barry as his own son. He bought Barry boxing gloves to learn to defend himself. He introduced Barry to local dishes of "dog meat (tough), snake meat (tougher), and roasted grasshopper (crunchy)." Barry learned Lolo's beliefs in Islam and animal powers and how to deal with endless streams of street beggars.

Indonesia proved a much different place from the beautiful land of aloha (a welcome greeting in Honolulu). Jakarta's downtown streets were a jumble of *becak*, or transport bicycles, motorcycles, carts, and a few cars. Barry saw waist-deep floods during rainy seasons. Other times, the beating sun drained rice and cassava fields bone dry. In streets and plains, Barry played with kites, watched cockfights, and tramped barefoot through muddy farms. At home, he took cold baths, battled mosquitoes, and used a hole in the ground for a toilet. Poverty, disease, and signs of deep divisions between rich and poor showed everywhere.

Lolo and Ann couldn't afford private school with other Americans for Barry. He attended local school with children of servants and farmers. It was a Catholic school in a Muslim country, giving Barry different understandings of religion and life. Within six months, Barry mastered Indonesia's language and customs.

Ann worried that the poor quality of education would limit her son's future. She sent for teacher supplies from the United States to build on his class work. Ann woke Barry at four in the morning every school day. Then she practiced lessons with her sleepy son for three hours before his class. Ann peppered each lesson with her sense of positive Midwestern values. She told him to be honest and fair, show good judgment, and always have faith in himself to chart his own future.

"If you want to grow into a human being, you're going to need some values," she told him.

After a couple of years, the added lessons were not enough for Ann. She feared Indonesia could be a dangerous place for her son. Moreover, she and Lolo were experiencing problems with their marriage.

Barry got a chance to explore the bustling streets of Jakarta after they moved to Indonesia so his mother could marry Lolo.

After four years in the country, Ann decided Barry should attend private school in Honolulu and live with Gramps and Toot. She and Maya, his baby sister, would follow soon.

School Years

At the age of ten, Barry returned to Honolulu. Getting off the plane, Barry noticed more gray hairs on Gramps and Toot. Other changes had occurred while he and his mother were gone. Gramps now sold life insurance, although without much success. Toot rose to bank vice president, the first woman to do so. The two led a quieter social life than they had four years earlier.

Barry's grandparents had moved into a two-bedroom apartment in a high-rise building. The apartment overlooked University Avenue and Diamond Head crater. The new building was in walking distance of Punahou School, Barry's new elementary and high school. The seventy-six-acre campus had been founded by Christian missionaries in 1841. It boasted a varied ethnic and religious population of students in kindergarten through twelfth grade. Barry's grandparents were proud to see their grandchild attend one of the largest and most respected private schools in the nation.

Barry entered fifth grade at the college prep school in the fall of 1971. He wore sandals from Indonesia and outdated clothes chosen by Gramps. Barry was one of the few new students and only one of two blacks in his grade. He felt totally out of place. After a few rocky months, he adjusted and gained friends. Barry never let on that questions about race and his parents gnawed at him.

"He was a good student. A nice, happy-go-lucky kid who knew how to stand up for himself," remembered Pal Eldredge, Barry's math and science teacher.

Barry spent seven years at Punahou. In the early days, his slightly round body still had some growing to do. Yet, he was a friendly boy who spoke out in class.

Barry (back row, third from left) moved back to Hawaii to attend fifth grade at Punahou School.

He seemed curious, always volunteering questions. He maintained a B-plus grade average, and he participated in many activities, some mischievous.

"Barry wrote his name in wet cement on campus by the cafeteria," said Eric Kusunoki, his homeroom teacher throughout high school. "Everyone knows who he is."

Basketball fever grabbed Barry during his high school years. His father, Barack, had sent him a basketball as a present. He bounced it on the way to school and in hallways going from class to class. He practiced

Barry, wearing number 23, goes up for a shot. Barry's love of playing basketball finally earned him a spot on his high school basketball team.

all the time. When others hid in the cafeteria during ninety-degree days, Barry shot hoops on the school's steamy black asphalt court.

"He was what we call a gym rat," explained coach Chris McLachlin. "He loved the game so much that he'd do anything to practice. He snuck past teachers when they opened the gym's locked doors. When no one was around, he broke into the gym."

Barry made the basketball team his last two years at Punahou. By then he came closer to his six-foot-two adult height. The team won second place in the state his first year on the team and first place during his senior year. Barry played forward on an exceptional team, which meant he competed for floor time during games. As Barry was the team's only left-hander, Coach McLachlin sent him out for sure whenever other left-handers played. Barry wore a number 23 jersey before Michael Jordan, the famous basketball star, made the number popular. Both players lived for the game.

"Barry was competitive but very intellectual as well. He understood the game and complicated plays," said Coach McLachlin. "Had it not been that cycle (of players), he would have been a star. I really admired the fact that he loved the game so much."

AS A CHILD, Barack wanted to be an astronaut, then an architect, and then a basketball player.

In high school, Barry lived with Ann and Maya. They took a small apartment on Beretania Street only a block from school. Ann returned to the university to obtain a master's degree in anthropology, the study of humans through time and place. She received grants to help pay her way, but money and time remained limited. Barry helped out whenever he could. He watched his sister, grocery shopped, washed clothes, and took a job scooping ice cream. When Ann needed to return to Indonesia for her fieldwork, Barry chose to live with his grandparents again. He thought he'd been uprooted enough.

Despite basketball and a good family and school, Barry appeared headed for trouble. Confusion over race stalked him. He and the few blacks who attended Punahou shared their anger over racial slights they experienced. A bad joke about Barry's color rubbing off that wasn't funny. Name-calling. A white woman's fearful

Barry's senior yearbook picture from Punahou School, the well-respected private school in Honolulu that he had attended since fifth grade

look when he followed her onto an elevator.

Bottled-up feelings and high school experimenting led Barry to try drugs. He stopped short of anything lasting and serious, and his schoolwork never suffered. But those days preyed on him later. "Junkie, pothead. That's where I'd been headed: the final, fatal role of the young would-be black man," Obama wrote.

To better understand what was happening to him, Barry read books. He studied famous authors to learn how they dealt with being black in a white-powered country. He worked to find his place in a family that was both black and white. He tried to accept himself. He tried not to feel so alone.

Off to College

Barry wasn't particularly interested in college. He chose Occidental College in Los Angeles because he had met a girl from there during the summer. The school of under two thousand students turned out to be beautiful. The California sun shone on the hillside campus with its palm trees, white buildings, and red-tiled roofs.

Occidental was where Barry tasted politics. Students on several campuses around the country spoke out against mistreatment of blacks in South Africa. They wanted their colleges to stop conducting business with the racist white government there. Barry gave an opening speech for a program to drum up interest in the cause at Occidental. For the first time, he felt the power of his words to change minds. He connected with an international black movement. As he claimed his voice and black identity, he reclaimed his Kenyan name, Barack.

> OBAMA HAS ALWAYS BEEN A BIG READER. He formed many of his ideas and goals after reading authors such as James Baldwin, Toni Morrison, and Ernest Hemingway.

After two years at Occidental, Barack became restless. He wrote to his father that he wanted to visit Kenya after graduation. Needing a change now, he took advantage of an exchange program between Occidental and Columbia University. In the fall of 1981, Barack moved to New York City and enrolled at Columbia. A different environment of honking horns, crowded streets and subways, and twenty-four-hour activity greeted him. Barack had never seen such a city. New Yorkers moved to their own beats–fast and faster.

Barack thrived on the change of pace. "I ran three miles a day and fasted on Sundays. For the first time, I applied myself to my studies and started keeping a journal of daily reflections and bad poetry," he wrote.

Two years later, Barack Obama graduated with a degree in political science, the study of politics, government, and how both work. By then he had received word that his father died in a car accident in Kenya. Obama put aside thoughts of visiting Africa–at least for the time being.

Pounding the Pavement

After college, Obama looked for a job as a community organizer. He wanted to promote civil rights at the grassroots, neighborhood level. When no organizing job developed, he took a position as research assistant for a large company. He had college loans to repay. He needed savings because organizers earned low salaries.

While Obama was at the company, Auma, his Kenyan half sister, called. She asked to visit him in New York. He knew Auma, who studied in Germany, only through a few letters. Meeting blood relatives excited him. Just before Auma's arrival, however, she called again. Their younger brother, David, had died in a motorcycle accident. She must return to Kenya instead. Barack tried to ease her sorrow. But he felt confused about his own feelings for a stepbrother he had never met.

In 1985 an organizing job opened in Chicago. Obama went to work for Developing Communities Project, a small group in the city's far South Side. The neighborhood had undergone a wave of plant closings and worker layoffs. Residents were left fighting just to survive. Obama hoped to organize them to push for improving their run-down living conditions.

Obama started the job filled with enthusiasm. But community organizing sometimes became a thankless

Residents walk past the LeClaire Courts housing project in Chicago. Obama hoped to help people in poorer communities improve their lives.

job. People living in projects scraped for enough money to fix their next meal. They didn't have time or energy to tackle broader social issues. Barack Obama refused to give up. He turned to churches to provide a base of support for his and the community's causes.

"He went from church to church, beating the pavement, trying to get every pastor in the community," the Reverend Alvin Love of Lilydale First Baptist Church told *StreetWise*. "This skinny, scrawny guy trying to find out how we can make the community better. He just walked the streets."

In the beginning, Obama called meetings where few people showed. Church leaders closed doors on his ideas. After several disappointments, Obama found some success. He helped bring job-training programs to poor neighborhoods. He gathered a busload of parents from a housing project and drove them to the downtown Chicago Housing Authority office. With Obama's support, they insisted on asbestos testing and removal for their apartments.

> OBAMA'S HEROES ARE Martin Luther King Jr., Mahatma Gandhi, and Cesar Chavez. They all believed in bringing about change through peaceful means.

With time, the people he helped, the close-knit neighborhoods, and the lakefront parks and museums grew on Obama. He often felt discouraged by the snail's pace of change. But this only fueled his desire to do more for the everyday folks he met. Obama realized that he had choices the others did not have. Maybe they came from the support of his family. Maybe they came from his being exposed to a larger world than a single run-down neighborhood. Maybe his choices stemmed from how smart and thoughtful he was. Whatever the reason, the more Obama met people in need, the more his desire to help them deepened.

Three years after arriving in Chicago, Obama applied to law schools to learn more tools for change. Several colleges accepted him. He chose Harvard University, his father's school.

Family in Kenya

Before leaving for school near Boston, Obama traveled to Kenya. He wanted to fill in the blanks about the father who had visited him only once—when Barack was a ten-year-old. All Barack remembered of the man was how he dropped into their lives, barked orders, and left forever. Before he left, Barack's father said he expected big things of his son. To the little boy, his father seemed an imposing man with bony knees and a deep, sure voice. Yet his hearty laugh and love of music filled a room.

BARACK WAS RAISED WITH KNOWLEDGE OF many religions. As an adult, he found great comfort in religion, and he says he has deep faith. He and his family belong to Chicago's Trinity United Church of Christ.

On his trip to Kenya, Obama met his grandmother, Onyango Obama, and two stepbrothers. Obama pieced together part of his past by connecting with family members he had never met.

Obama wanted to understand more about this mystery man. He wanted to learn about the land of his roots.

In Kenya Obama toured the capital of Nairobi. Peddlers in the old marketplace hawked wooden trinkets and jewelry. Women wrapped in bright cloth with shaven heads and beaded earrings carried goods on their heads. He visited aunts, uncles, and cousins on the outskirts of the city. He met his Kenyan grandmother in Kisumu, a sleepy town on the savanna along Lake

Victoria. Auma introduced Barack to his stepbrothers Roy and Bernard, each from a different marriage.

Over the next month, Barack Obama pieced together his African history. He learned about his father's high-level government job as an economist. He heard about his fall from grace after he bucked corrupt officials. With each story, Barack understood more about his father's princely pride and great generosity. Then he cried at his father's grave. He made peace with the man and larger-than-life stories from his childhood. Barack Obama left Kenya with a stronger feeling of himself and where he belonged in the world.

New Directions

Obama entered Harvard University in the fall of 1988. "On first impression, he seemed older than he was," recalled Kenneth Mack, former classmate and current Harvard assistant professor. "I thought of him as a black guy with a Midwestern accent. But he seemed experienced in the world in ways some of us weren't. He spoke well and concisely in a way that seemed wise and broad-minded."

The first year of law school required lots of studying. To unwind, Obama shot baskets as he had always done. Basketball star Michael Jordan, number 23, became his symbol of focus, hard work, and competition.

At the end of his first year, Obama made *Harvard Law Review*. Although a journal for legal scholars, many considered the *Review* the highest honor for law students. Candidates submitted their grades and a writing sample. Those selected became editors who wrote or edited articles for the monthly journal. After a year on the job, all the editors chose Obama as president of the review, the first African American to receive the honor.

In 1989 Obama was selected for the *Harvard Law Review*. A year later, he was elected its president.

The announcement produced a flurry of media attention. A publishing company contracted with Obama to write the story of his life. Doors opened to leading law firms.

The summer before graduation, Barack clerked at a large Chicago law firm. He discovered that he disliked the cutthroat atmosphere of high-powered corporate law for wealthy clients. But he did like Chicago. He felt at home here. After Harvard, Obama returned to Chicago to look for work.

Part of the reason for Obama's return involved a new woman in his life. Michelle Robinson was the lawyer responsible for showing him around the firm that summer. Robinson was a tall, noble-looking Yale graduate who received her law degree from Harvard before Obama did. Michelle sounded thoughtful, bright, and totally frank, a perfect match for Barack. The two married in 1991.

Michelle Robinson's Harvard yearbook photo. Barack and Michelle met in Chicago and fell in love.

The couple moved into the mixed-race Hyde Park neighborhood on Chicago's South Side. Obama completed his book there. Then he joined a small firm that focused on civil rights. His legal cases involved job discrimination and low-income housing. He worked to improve public health and the environment.

In 1992 Obama added Illinois Project Vote to his workload. Under his direction, the project registered 150,000 new voters from poor neighborhoods to give them a voice in elections. Evenings, Obama taught classes in constitutional law at the University of Chicago.

"He stood out in everything he did. He worked in court. He wrote briefs," said his law firm boss Judson Miner. "Barack is an extraordinarily talented person with an extraordinary set of values in every respect. It was clear early on that he was going to be pressured at some point to jump into government or politics."

Public Office

Obama made no secret of wanting to run for public office. He mentioned the subject to friends at Harvard. He talked about it while at the law firm. In 1996 State Senator Alice Palmer handed Obama his chance to become an elected politician. She decided to run for Congress and drafted him to fill her slot as state senator. Palmer's Thirteenth District included wealthier blacks and whites from the University of Chicago area, where Barack and Michelle lived. It also extended into the poor, mainly black regions farther south, where Obama had worked during his organizing days.

As Obama's campaign fired up, Palmer changed her mind. She had lost the primary election to represent her party and wanted her job back. Obama refused, saying she promised not to run. Besides, his campaign was already hot. Obama's workers challenged Palmer's petitions to run. The resulting battle caused Palmer to withdraw from the race. The setback ended her career in politics.

Obama wound up winning the race for state senator. But the situation caused hard feelings among black power brokers. Many felt he should have stepped aside. Palmer was older and didn't have many more chances to serve, whereas he did.

Four years later, Obama faced a similar situation. He believed that the sitting U.S. representative, Bobby Rush, wasn't doing enough for his district. Barack jumped into the race to unseat the four-time winner. This time, Obama lost. Rush whipped him two to one in the primary. Obama finally learned his lesson. He vowed to take politics slower. He had a lot to learn about state government before he tackled national politics. The Illinois senator focused on improving conditions for his South Side supporters. Still, the two races hinted at how competitive—and impatient—Obama really was.

For his seven years in the Illinois Senate, Obama fought on behalf of working families. He chaired the public health and welfare committee. In this position, he

Obama argues during a debate on legislation about immigrant driver's licenses at the state capitol in Springfield, Illinois, on November 6, 2003. He served in the Illinois State Senate for seven years before being elected to a national office.

introduced more than 780 bills. About 280 became law.

Under Obama's leadership, state government expanded insurance programs for twenty thousand additional children and sixty-five thousand more families in Illinois. He helped reduce taxes for working families. He ushered in a bill to further protect women from abuse. His boldest move, however, involved another law-enforcement bill. He led the call for groundbreaking rules that required police to videotape questioning of murder suspects.

To accomplish so much, Obama needed the respect of other state representatives. He had a gift for reaching out to opponents to find agreement. "What drove him was policy issues," said Miner. "But he realized that government involves compromise. Barack was so talented that he compromised from a position of strength."

Going National

In April 2003, Illinois's U.S. senator, Peter Fitzgerald, declined to run for a second term. Barack saw his chance to enter national politics. He was ready to try another election for national office. This time, Obama quickly shot ahead of others in his party. He easily beat six opponents in the primary, with 53 percent of the vote.

"We confounded a lot of odds that said that whites won't vote for blacks, or those in suburbs won't vote for a city guy or downstate people won't vote for folks from upstate," Obama told a PBS reporter.

After the primary, Republican rivals self-destructed. The front-runner, Jack Ryan, withdrew from the race over a family scandal. Fearful state Republicans brought in a black out-of-state former ambassador named Alan

During a televised debate for the Illinois U.S. senate race, Obama (left) and Alan Keyes (right) argued the issues. Obama's positive campaign and powerful Democratic National Convention speech gave him an edge over Keyes.

Keyes. Keyes tore through the state like a bulldog. He attacked Obama on all levels—his ideas, his character, anything he said.

Obama stuck to running a positive race. He spoke of hope and unity. His motto was "Yes, we can." Compared with Keyes's rants, Obama seemed better than reasonable. He was awesome. Obama connected with all kinds of people. He already proved he could get jobs done in state government.

In March 2005, Julian Bond of the NAACP presented Obama with the Chairman's Award for recognition of special achievement and distinguished service. The NAACP honored Obama with two different awards in 2005.

Then came Obama's stirring speech at the Democratic National Convention. His star power soared. Keyes didn't have a chance after that. Obama's campaign raised more than $14 million, a large amount for an unknown. Basketball legend Michael Jordan alone donated $10,000. Obama pulled far ahead in the polls. He was so popular everywhere that he spoke at rallies in other states on behalf of local candidates.

Obama won a sweeping victory against Keyes, with 70 percent of the vote. He became only the fifth black U.S. senator in history. Invitations poured in for him to speak at various groups. Many gave him awards, such as the NAACP (National Association for the Advancement of Colored People) Fight for Freedom Award. Obama's publisher offered him a three-book deal worth $1.9 million.

"It took a lot of blood, sweat, and tears to get to where we are today, but we have just begun," Obama wrote in a blog. Supporters agreed. Many expressed great hopes for his future. Some called him the Great Black Hope, or a rising star. Internet sites offered "Obama for '08 President" bumper stickers and posters with "Obama in 2012." People in Obama's father's province in Kenya expressed similar high hopes. African parents named babies Barack, after him. They held Obama up as a role model for older kids and named an elementary school after him.

As junior Illinois senator and a newcomer, however, Obama ranked ninety-ninth out of one hundred in the Senate pecking order. His ability to effect change would be limited, at least for now. First, he had to set up his tiny office in the basement and "learn to find his way around the building."

To help him stay grounded, Obama recalled his life journey to the Senate. He marveled at how a boy raised in two countries with roots in a third and who attended schools run by three different religions could have come so far. But then what better way is there to understand what is important to every group of people?

OBAMA IS MORE OF A REGULAR GUY THAN MOST PEOPLE IN POLITICS, possibly because he is not as wealthy. In his free time, he reads, takes walks, and goes to the movies. His main household jobs include shopping and taking out the garbage.

Obama enjoys time with his wife, Michelle, and his two daughters, Natasha (left) and Maile Ann (right).

Still, the pressure for Obama to produce in the future is overwhelming. Only time will tell what the "skinny kid with a funny name" can accomplish. Many people worry that the spotlight will spoil him. He will forget why he originally entered politics.

Many more, like Judson Miner, disagree. They know that Obama is the real deal.

"He has good judgment. He will not let things that matter the least get in the way of those that matter most," Miner said. "Barack wants to make a difference."

IMPORTANT DATES

1961   Born on August 4 in Honolulu, Hawaii

1967   Moves with his mother and new stepfather
            to Jakarta, Indonesia

1971   Returns to Hawaii and enrolls at Punahou
            School

1979   Graduates from Punahou School and enters
            Occidental College in Los Angeles

1981   Switches to Columbia University in New
            York City

1983   Graduates from Columbia University with a
            degree in political science

1985   Begins a three-year job as community
            organizer in Chicago

1988   Starts Harvard Law School in Cambridge,
            Massachusetts

1990   Elected the first black president of *Harvard
            Law Review*

1991	Graduates from Harvard Law School magna cum laude, with highest honors. Marries Michelle Robinson
1992	Joins a Chicago law firm to work on civil rights cases
1995	Publishes *Dreams from My Father* with Three Rivers Press
1996	Wins election for Illinois state senator
1999	Maile Ann, the Obama's first child, is born
2000	U.S. representative from Illinois, Bobby Rush, beats Obama in the primary by a two-to-one margin.
2002	Second daughter, Natasha, is born
2004	Elected U.S. Senator from Illinois, becoming the fifth African American in history to join the Senate
2005	Receives the NAACP Fight for Freedom Award as well as its Chairman's Award

GLOSSARY

aloha: "love," used as a greeting or farewell in Hawaii

anthropology: study of humans through time and place

becak: public transport bicycles

cassava: plant grown for its root that is made into a starch for pudding and tapioca

gibbon: small ape of Southeast Asia

multiethnic: refers to people from different countries

poi: taro root that is cooked and pounded into paste for Hawaiian food

political science: study of politics and government and how both work

politics: art or science of government

primary: election to see who will represent a group of voters in a final election

sashimi: Japanese dish of sliced raw fish

FURTHER READING

No other biographies of Barack Obama for young readers exist at this time. The following websites include interesting information about Barack Obama:

Barak Obama Official Blog & Daily Campaign Diary
(2004 campaign)
http://www.obamablog.com

Barak Obama U.S. Senator for Illinois
http://www.obama.senate.gov/contact

ACKNOWLEDGMENTS

I want to thank Barack Obama for writing about his youth in the adult autobiography, *Dreams from My Father: A Story of Race and Inheritance.* Several people helped me enrich his story with their own memories of Barack. I appreciate the time Professor Kenneth Mack and Kelly Shapiro, Harvard Law School; Judson Miner; Pam Towill, the Hawaii State Library; and Pal Eldredge, Eric Kusunoki, Laurel Husain, and Chris McLachlin, Punahou School, took to share their impressions of Barack with me. In addition, I used articles in magazines such as *Time, Savoy, Harvard Magazine,* and *The New Yorker*; articles in newspapers such as the *Honolulu Advertiser, Star Bulletin, Chicago Sun-Times, Chicago Tribune,* and *StreetWise;* and many websites about Indonesia, Hawaii, and the schools Barack attended.

INDEX

Page numbers in *italics* refer to illustrations.

Africa, 9, 12, 27
Auma (half sister), 27, 32

Boston, 30

Chicago, 28, *28*, 30, 34–35
Chicago Housing Authority, 29
Columbia University, 26

Democratic Party, 7
Developing Communities Project, 28
Dreams from My Father, 18, *18*
Dunham, Madelyn (grandmother), 10
Dunham, Stanley (grandfather), 10
Dunham, Stanley Ann (mother), 8,
    12–14, 24

Harvard Law Review, 32–33
Harvard University, 15, 30, 32, 34,
    35
Hawaii, 8, 10, 11, 15, *16*, 20
Hawaiians, 11
Honolulu, 8, 10–11, *11*, 20
Hyde Park, 35

Illinois, 7, 37, 41
Illinois Project Vote, 35

Jakarta, Indonesia, 17–18, *20*

Kansas, *9*, 9–10

Kenya, 9, 12, 15, 26, 27, 28, 31–32,
    41
Keyes, Alan, 38–39, *39*, 40
Kisumu, Kenya, 31

Lake Victoria (Kenya), 12, *13*
Lolo (stepfather), 17, 18, 19
Los Angeles, 26

Maya (sister), 20, 24

Nairobe, 12, 30
New York City, 26

Obama, Barack, *25, 33, 37*
    as Barry, 15–26
    basketball, 22–23, *23*, 32, 40
    birth of, 8
    campaign for U.S. Senate, 38–41
    childhood of, 8, 15, 16–27
    at Democratic National
    Convention, *6, 7*, 40
    as editor of *Harvard Law Review,*
        32–33, *33*
    education of, 19, 20–21, *22*,
        25–27, 32–34
    entering politics, 35–36
    family, *42*
    marriage of, 34
    meaning of name, 9
    NAACP award, *40*

parents of, 9–10, 12–16
  as state senator, 36–37
Obama, Barack (father) 9, 12–15
Obama, David (half brother), 27
Obama, Hussein Onyango (grandfather), 12
Obama, Onyanga (grandmother), *31*
Occidental College, 26

Palmer, Alice, 35–36
Punahou School, 21–24, *22*

Robinson, Michelle (wife), 34, *34*

Seattle, 10
South Africa, 26
South Side (Chicago), 36

Texas, 13
Thirteenth District, 35

University of Chicago, 35
University of Hawaii, 12, 14, *14*